WHEN LITTLES ARE LOUD

*Maximizing the Moments
without Drowning in Chaos*

*By Val Harrison, The Practically
Speaking MOM*

CHAPTER 1: LIFE WITH LITTLES; BONDING OVER A LITTLE MOM-CRAZY

Where kids abound, so do unpredictable moments. If you're the parent of very many littles (you know, the loud but small tikes who roam your home), I can guess that you share some of my same crazy history! I think it's time for you and I to bond over a little bit of mom-crazy that is brought on by a house full of littles! Can you identify with any of these moments from my life?

*Changed a diaper of an interesting color and realized the baby had been eating a crayon.

*Had a line at least three children deep waiting to talk to me or ask a question.

*Started the washing machine, put in soap, and ran the whole cycle before I realized I didn't remember to put the dirty clothes into the washer.

*Had a pre-schooler try to change an infant dirty diaper because she was "trying to help."

*Had a bar of soap or any interesting item flushed down the toilet that wasn't supposed to be flushed down the toilet.

(Do you happen to know how many gallons of hot water it takes to melt down a bar of soap enough to get it to pass on through the plumbing? I don't either because after 80 gallons we stopped trying and took off the toilet. In the pipe we found six Legos, one Matchbox car, a few unidentifiable objects, and that pesky bar of soap).

*Re-put in the laundry detergent for a second time... and forgot the clothes for a second time.

*And a third time. (At this point I gave up on getting any laundry done that day).

*Got everyone ready to go except for one shoe and had all family members looking for said shoe for at least 20 minutes until we gave up and headed to the van, only to find out it was already in the van!

 *Announced to my children, "Mommy's going into the bathroom. Unless you're bleeding, or the house is on fire, don't knock on the door. I'll be back in a minute," and within three seconds of entering the bathroom I hear the first knock.

Parenting toddlers is exhausting!

If any of those scenarios sound like your life, then you're the parent of littles! For being the tiniest bodies in the house, it's rather ironic that they can be so LOUD.

How are we to get anything done with the other kids when the littlest of the bunch seem to demand our constant attention?!

Well, after seven of my own children and now enjoying some grand babies, I've had a few opportunities to make mistakes, overcorrect, try again, and eventually learn what is important, what works, and what doesn't, when raising toddlers and preschoolers.

_____

_____

OUR FAMILY:

Seven Children including two married daughters and two grandsons. (back row), three sons and a daughter, Abby (front row), youngest daughter, Emma (back row).

CHAPTER 2: FIRST THINGS FIRST

Your little guy might be young, but it is NOT too early for you to be intentionally shaping his habits, character, and living out God's will for your child's life. When I look at my kids' lives, my number one above- all- else prayer for them is that they would live each day in God's will for that day, be in the habit of living intentionally, and then as adults that they would be in the habit of daily seeking God's direction in living out His calling for their uniquely fashioned-by-God life. Our Heavenly Father loves your kids even more than you do and He has designed their days to be so much more than you could ask or imagine!

Place their days and their futures in HIS HANDS and then partner with Him to do everything you can to help them reach the place of abiding in His will.

THIS BOOK IS MOSTLY PRACTICAL SOLUTIONS
FOR SPECIFIC TODDLER/PRESCHOOL ISSUES, BUT
FIRST IN THIS CHAPTER WE'RE GOING TO BE MORE
PHILOSOPHICAL. MY GUESS IS THAT YOU'D RATHER
BE JUMPING RIGHT INTO THE PRACTICAL IDEAS AND
SYSTEMS FOR SUCCESS WITH YOUR LITTLE, BUT CAN
WE JUST TAKE A FEW PAGES TO GET PERSPECTIVE
FIRST?

Ephesians 3:18-20 "And may you have the power to understand, as all God's people should, how wide, how long, how high, and how deep his love is. May you experience the love of Christ, though it is too great to understand fully. Then you will be made complete with all the fullness of life and power that comes from God. Now to Him who is able to do immeasurably more than we could ask or imagine, according to His power that is at work within us." (NLT)

When I was in my early years of motherhood with three children five and under, I was ready to get a game plan for what success would look like for me and my children-determining what I was aiming for in motherhood. Each day was busy and tiring where every bit of my energy went into nurturing Tori, Becca, and Nathan. **I realized that I didn't want to just be going through the routine of our days -feeding, playing, cleaning, sleeping, repeat. No, I wanted each day to be an investment in their future – to develop their hearts, souls, minds, and bodies with a clear focus on the long term. I took some time to develop my big picture goals for my kids.**

The image on the following page is what I developed from that time of self-examination and goal-setting. Now twenty years later, I have continued to use this same chart to keep me focused on what really matters in our daily lives.

This chart is a ladder with the top rung of the ladder being "God's Will for My Child." It is a modified "hierarchy of needs" ladder. You start at the bottom of the ladder each day with your child and work your way up the ladder.

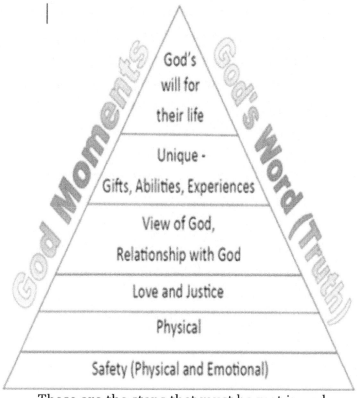

These are the steps that must be met in order to truly be on track with God's will for their life. This ladder also works from a long-term perspective – that we need to get each step of the ladder in place and healthy if we want our kids to be the place in life where they are discovering God's will for their life on their own someday. I'm going to explain this chart further but take a look at it first.

The 1st three rungs are the first three things to think about filling up in our littles each morning – safety, physical, and love & justice needs.

God Moments throughout Each Day

God Moments:

A daily lifestyle of seeing God at work in our
lives and in His creation, being tuned-in to
"God with us." To achieve this lifestyle of
seeing God and hearing from God in our daily
lives, we must intentionally train our children
to see and hear God at work in our lives.

God's Truth throughout Each Day

God's Word (Truth)

INCORPORATE GOD'S WORD INTO YOUR CHILD'S
DAILY LIFE. BIBLICALLY-BASED MUSIC, BOOKS,
DVDS, AND CONVERSATION CAN ALL BE
SELECTED WITH THIS IN MIND. ALSO SET ASIDE
A TIME EACH DAY AS A SPECIAL FEW MINUTES
OF LEARNING GOD'S WORD TOGETHER WITH
YOUR CHILD. LITTLES LOVE TO BE GIVEN HAND
MOTIONS TO LEARN A BIBLE VERSE AND CAN BE
A SPECIAL TIME EACH DAY FOR LEARNING A
BIBLE VERSE WITH MOM.

My chart is adapted from something I had been taught in one of my college psychology classes, Maslow's Hierarchy of Needs. Maslow believed the highest goal for a person was self-actualization and that there were four rungs on a ladder leading up to that goal (physical needs, safety needs, social needs, esteem needs).

While I respectfully disagree with the details of much of his perspective, it did help me to analyze my own life and that of my children to help figure out what I believe the rungs of life really are – what are the needs that must be met at each level and how does one level impact the next. In this book I'm not going to go into a detailed look at my entire chart or how I apply it, but I do want us to focus for a few minutes on the first three rungs of the ladder to God's will for your child's life.

When our children are in their earliest years, the first three rungs (Safety Needs, Physical Needs, Love and Justice) are all the first and most vital concerns that we parents need to be meeting each day. That's probably not a

surprise to you. I'm sure you consider these three areas all day every day for your children. I found it helpful when raising littles to see this as a checklist to begin each day. I wanted to move them as high up that ladder each day as possible.

Rung # 1: Safety Needs (both physical and emotional protection from harmful forces).

Protecting our children means more than just locking front doors and using car seats. It also includes protecting their **minds** from harmful images on screens, protecting their **emotions** from inconsistent boundaries, or from the minefield of **spiritual** damage caused by a hypocritical parent who isn't seeking God's best for her own life but expecting it in their child's life. Ouch, that stings a little to me. **I want to add here, that usually I bring up tough things when it is a personal mistake I have already made and am hoping to save you from the same pain.**

I pray that you will take some time to evaluate how SAFE your home truly is for your child's mind, heart, and spirit. Are there some improvements that you may need to make in your child's home to protect them better?

My grandson Asher

Let me just be honest with you here. I did well at providing for the physical safety of my kids, but sometimes I didn't do as well on some other important aspects of safety. There were times that if I was tired, I would change the boundaries because I didn't feel like enforcing them that day. This led, in those seasons of our life, to much more chaos in our home because I hadn't been consistent in what I would and wouldn't allow them to do. **Once I learned the importance of keeping boundaries consistent no matter what, the less tug-of-war there was between me enforcing rules and the littles following them, because they knew the boundaries were not shifting and were non-negotiable.**

I also struggled with a grouchy or sarcastic attitude that was definitely not producing feelings of safety in my children. As God began to show me the ugliness of my attitude and the effects it was having on my kids, the guilt was huge. I pray that you'll learn from my mistakes and get a handle on your emotions to give them a more predictable environment where they will thrive emotionally, mentally, physically, and spiritually.

When Littles are Loud

Let's say you're at a job where your boss is constantly adjusting the rules based on his feelings and he is often grouchy and sarcastic in his responses to you. How safe do you feel in your job? Does it increase your creativity or stifle it? Does it motivate you to perform well? Our children are even less resilient than we are in withstanding these inconsistencies in the environment. Begin praying that God would show you the ways you need to improve your child's safety needs.

Rung #2: Physical Needs (hunger, thirst, sleep, cleanliness, comfortable environment)

I've figured something out over the years. There are certain personality types that are very high physical needs people, no matter their age. If this type person is hot, cold, hungry, thirsty, or tired, their cranky-side shows up quick! Certainly, every person has physical needs that are of vital importance, but these special High Physical Needs Individuals are *easily derailed* by their physical needs. So, tune in to your youngsters' physical condition to keep them at prime positioning for moving up that ladder to God's will for their day! **They will learn more thoroughly, retain information more effectively, receive correction more peacefully, and so much more when their physical needs have been well managed.**

My philosophy is that the earlier in the day that I can get them moved up the ladder of needs, the richer our days will be as we'll be reaching the higher rungs heading toward God's will. Of course, some of the things on my chart are not fully attainable when our children are very young but every day we're developing a way of life that leads to the fullness of God's goodness and blessings or leads us away from them. Let's start those good habits early or else we are surely living out bad ones!

Rung #3: <u>Love and Justice Needs</u> (Showing my child I love and adore him or her, and that I'm so glad to be together **while also** being consistent with boundaries and enforcing my word and stepping in when there is an unjust situation).

You may have heard of the series of books on the Five Love Languages. There's a concept I gleaned from <u>The Five Love Languages of Children</u> by Gary Chapman and Ross Campbell. (Also see <u>How to Really Love Your Child</u> by Ross Campbell for more on the idea of a love tank). The concept is that there is a "Love Tank" that each of us possesses, and when that love tank is full, we are at our best-we learn more, more easily, we are more creative, and more resilient when our love tank is full! That concept has helped me so many times throughout my years of parenting. And on the flipside, my biggest regrets as a mom have also been connected to the ways I unknowingly would deplete my child's love tank through my negative or smart-aleck attitude.

Moms, every age, even teenagers, need their love tank filled up. Here's the key to remember: FILL THE YOUNGEST LOVE TANK FIRST. A child with a full love tank can play on their own better, be less clingy, and have more peace.

One way I did this as a homeschool mom of littles was to schedule five minutes at the top of every hour with the toddler in a focused one-on-one time with them. Then this bought me some minutes of focused time with an older student to go over their assignment, etc. Certainly, after the few minutes of focused time with each of your tots they still need supervision, but **they are far less needy because they aren't running on emotional fumes** anymore. <u>The thing with littles is that</u>

<u>their tanks empty quickly so they need refills far more often than olders, when it comes to mom-time.</u> Again, five minutes at the top of every hour for focused love-filling time with your little is a great habit to develop.

Here's a few more love-tank-filling ideas, from my blog, The Practically Speaking MOM. These ideas are not just about littles:

Top Five Daily Ways to Show
Love to Your Child or
Grandchild

1. Full Eye-contact Smile

Have you ever walked into a room and someone's eyes, countenance, and spirit just lit up when they saw you? It probably hasn't happened too much as those kinds of experiences are rare and wonderful. Doesn't it make you feel amazing to know that someone likes your presence that much? This is the kind of message we want to try to give our children daily. This includes giving them a  genuine smile with full eye contact. It's a good goal to envision yourself having such a strong feeling of love when you smile at them that your eye sparkles with the delight and happiness that their presence creates. I know this may sound silly (it feels silly to write it also), but the truth is that it is incredibly stabilizing to our souls to know that someone completely adores us. Our Heavenly Father does, of course, but we are our child's first understanding and comprehension of what unconditional love looks like and feels like and as we display it well to them, they will better be able to comprehend the boundless love of God towards them.

I have to confess that it wasn't until our last child that I learned to literally envision myself having a eye that sparkles when my daughter walks in the room. For some reason, that silly little goal transformed my ability to set aside whatever I might be feeling or going through or being distracted by. When she would walk into the room, I would just seek to get a sparkle in my eye about the joy I feel from seeing her come in the room. Small mental goals like that can really help us overcome even our own emotions. Give it a try!

2. <u>Laugh Together</u>

Getting a little one to laugh is pretty simple. In fact, if you laugh, they'll pretty much laugh, no matter the reason. In the early years, tickling them or reading them a silly story are great ways to laugh together, or my favorite of all with a little is to chase them. It's so fun to just pretend you're trying to "get them." I love hearing a little toddler squeal with delight as they try to hurry away. Good laughs all around from a good chase!

However, it gets more challenging to get your child to laugh as they get older. For an elementary age child, some more things to try are *talking with a funny voice, *showing them a funny picture or telling a joke, *doing something unexpected, such as jumping out and scaring them. Partly it depends on your child's personality as to what they see as "funny" and what is just "annoying." One of the great privileges of parenthood is to become a student of your child – figure out the uniqueness's of his or her personality and perspective.

And then there are "middle years" love tanks. What makes a middle schooler laugh? Pretty much anything that you think is ridiculous. Okay, that technically may be an exaggeration on my part, but truly, middle schoolers are going through such change and self-evaluation that they have a hard time knowing how they feel about many aspects of life, including deciding whether something is humorous, hilarious, or terrible. Keep trying to laugh with them, though, because they really need some comic relief from the stressors they're dealing with internally.

A pretty reliable form of fun with middle and high school age kids is to develop some "inside jokes." Our family has bonded over our favorite movies or experiences and sharing a line from a movie or from a good memory brings some quick comedy to the fast-paced routines of a busy family.

In short, laughter creates bonds. The more you laugh with your child the closer you will become. I must confess, I am not a fun or funny person. This one is very hard for me. I am gradually getting better at it. I will say, that I can think of two different times when one of my kids was a teenager and we were clashing a lot, that taking them out for the day (an unplanned time of missing school and just going on a day time parent/teen date and being light-hearted and silly) really helped a lot. Don't underestimate the power of a laugh! (Playing a game together is another great way to bond and make memories.)

3. Physical Affection

A squishy hug (no stiff or floppy hugs, they don't count), scratching their back, even a poke in the ribs, or messing with their hair can make your child feel like you enjoy being with them and that you love them so much.

Now that some of my children are grown, my husband has gotten into a habit, when we are saying "goodbye" to each of our grown daughters, - he always gets face to face with each daughter, takes her face in his hands and kisses her forehead. Just a small gesture, but I can see it on each daughter's face while he does that that it gives her such comfort and confidence to have Daddy's affection. One of my grown daughters is a mom and the other is a youth director, yet they both are so filled by getting that precious moment of Dad's physical affection. It doesn't matter how old they get, our children long for our love, approval, and affection.

4. Verbal Blessing

There are so many great ways to verbally love on your child! Giving her a nickname (well, one she likes), giving her verbal praise for attitudes and actions in which she has recently displayed good character, letting him know specific ways that you are proud of him...

these are all ways to verbally bless your child. Of course, when you're giving a verbal blessing to a toddler, the message needs to be much less complex, such as, "Jamey is such a good boy. He always is careful and brave" or "Jamey, we love you so much!"

Another concept related to this that I mention in my book <u>Wearing All Your Hats without Wearing Out</u>, is the concept of being a VISIONARY in your child's life – help them see what they cannot yet see in themselves by painting a picture of your child's qualities that you see in him that is going to shape his future.

In fact, in the book, I suggest that being a <u>Visionary</u> in your child's life is one of the four main roles of a parent. An example of this that I might say to my high school son might be, "Andrew, God has given you such a calm strength in making decisions. I can't wait to see how God is going to help you lead others with this quality." Or to my college son I might say, "Josh, I have come to have a lot of confidence in your ability to make objective decisions in tough situations, no matter what you may be feeling on the inside, so I know you're going to handle this decision well also." Or to my thirteen-year-old daughter I may say, "Abby, you have such a compassionate heart and I know that many people will be blessed by your caring for them in their times of need." You're setting in your child's mind a vision of a good future.

I'm sure you've heard the phrase, "self-fulfilling prophecy." Well, it really is human nature to become what we believe we are. **Your child's future has everything to do with who they believe they are and, as our child's main visionary, we have the greatest influence over how they perceive themselves.** This is why we as parents need to give careful consideration to the labels that we give, or others give, to our children. Our children don't need to know every clinical label that has been assigned to them. I'm sure for some children it is helpful to know such information but for some of them, the label becomes a definition in their mind – a definition of who they are and all the limitations that are characterized by that label. As your child's primary Visionary, it is critical that you understand the power of the words spoken over your child. Sometimes we are unintentionally being a negative visionary in our child's life. Even little negative nicknames may feel endearing at the time, but it really can affect the child's self-perception as he or she grows.

Sadly, I speak from experience on this issue. I used to "negative joke" regularly with some of my children and I thought it was just being light-hearted and even bonding, but this was actually weighing them down emotionally and I didn't realize it. By the time I realized the affect it was having there definitely was no adequate way to re-do it, but only to do my best to restore and repair. Regret is one of the worst things in all of life! What's better than regret, a lot better than regret, is intentionality with our words. Proverbs 18:21 says that "death and life are in the power of the tongue, and those who love it will eat its fruits," (ESV). **The words we choose to say to and about our children will bring life or death to their spirits. Choose your words wisely.**

5. Verbalize Your Thoughts about Your Child

When you hear that someone has been thinking of you, how does that make you feel? Cherished? Valued? Loved? Our children need to know we're thinking of them. Here are some ways to verbalize this:

"Today I was just thinking about how thankful I am that God brought you to our family."

"I have been contemplating a decision about something, and I'd really value your thoughts on this issue."

"I've really been missing you today, so I wanted to check-in with you and see how you're doing."

"When I spend time praying for you today, is there anything specific that you'd like me to be praying about?"

"Recently, I have been thinking about all the ways you are a blessing to our family. Thank

you for your love and smile and caring that you give to all of us. You are such a valuable part of our family."

That was a blog post about multiple ages and can be found on my website, www.PracticallySpeakingMOM.com

Let's look now at some specifics of filling love tanks in the younger years:

5min Toddler Tank Refill Time @ the top of every hour

Filling love tanks had to be a very intentional endeavor for me because I'm not naturally a soft, gentle, patient, cuddly- type person. I'm more of a task-management type. I literally had to set the timer each hour during the day. The top of the hour was for five minutes of focused, one-on-one, quality time with my toddler. Yes, I had been spending the entire time with him already, but I was thinking about this or that, or training on an issue, or trying to achieve something. It took me a long time to learn the lesson that my kids needed to see the sparkle in my eye that comes from how much I adore them. *My greatest regret is that in my earlier parenting years I was often so caught up in trying to make sure they were good that I failed to show them that they were* _**unconditionally treasured.**_ The most filling-up type of love is letting them see that you are experiencing great joy just by being together.

Now, I should mention here, that while my weakness was to focus more on the character than the affection, there are parents who have the opposite tendency- to put affection ahead of character development. Both affection and character development are essential to healthy development for kids. Figure out which you are weak in giving, as a parent, and get a game plan for fixing that weakness. Your kids deserve both affection and boundaries.

The special five minutes might be reading a book to them, singing to them, showing them something from God's creation that they've never known about before, or cuddling on the couch while I tell them the ways that I see they are growing and doing well.

When my house was full of very young children (I'm the mom of four daughters and three sons) and they all had big love tanks that needed filling, I taught them that when it is a Mommy/Child special time, not to interrupt. To do this, I used a homemade sign and a timer. Toddlers got an official "Mom-

Elementary:
Mom & Me Time
Once a Day

and-Me" every hour while the elementary children got it once a day. Kids knew that if I had the sign set up and timer going, it meant that I was having some special time with one of the children (I could be right in the same room with the others, but the sign would be up and they knew to wait until the timer went off before they should interrupt with a question or a need). This made the one child I was giving time to feel very treasured. Since each wanted the other siblings to honor his or her special time, each learned to honor the other kids' special times also. This process was so important in our home to get all those love tanks filled.

In John Eldredge's book <u>The Way of the Wild Heart</u> (a book I can't recommend enough as it really helped to heal some wounds that my husband had from earlier years in his life and helped my husband and I to make several important improvements in our parenting), John talks about the stages of a boy's life. The first stage is that of the "Beloved Son" and the principle for this stage is essential in both boys and girls. In this stage, the child needs to know that he is adored by his parents, loved beyond measure.

To my shame, there were some difficult years in mine and my children's lives where I was not good at "adoring" them -- making them feel "beloved." I could tell you there were reasons going on in my life that were keeping me from handling love-tank filling adequately, but the fact is that no matter the reason, the harm still happened, and it meant that I had some children with wounded hearts that needed mending. Don't make the mistake I made. I'd love to be able to report that I never fail in this crucial role of showing my kids how priceless they are in my eyes but, as a non-touchy-feely

type, I do still struggle with effectively and clearly sending that message to my kids daily. You remember that, at the beginning of this book, I said we should bond over some similar mom-history. Well, may I implore you to NOT share the history with me of regretting that you didn't, at times, give them the most needed love-tank filling of all -- giving them "the blessing," even on their most difficult days. (See <u>The Blessing</u> by John Trent and Gary Smalley). Fill their love tanks and every single day look into their eyes and let them know you adore them.

Now that most of my kids are older (four of them are grown and moved out) and don't want or need *as much* one-on-one time with me, I have plenty of opportunity for uninterrupted time with my youngest, so we don't have need for a sign and timer. This will vary based on the ages and number of your children.

More on the importance of Love & Justice

If you take a look back at the chart of the "Ladder to God's Will for Your Child's Life," there were TWO words on Rung #3 – Love and Justice. We spent a lot of time on love. We can't move past this rung on the ladder until we take a close look at Justice.

What do I mean by "justice" and why does it hold equal importance with love, when it comes to raising our children? **By "justice," I am referring to the quality of maintaining an environment that is fair and honest, with clear boundaries, consequences, and blessings in which the parent gives truthful, impartial decisions.** Think of a judge (the men and women in our governmental system entrusted with the important task of determining appropriate consequences for actions, judging those actions in a fair and equal way). Do you want to stand before a judge who is continually changing the rules - sometimes rewarding a certain behavior and the next time punishing that same behavior? Of course, we would never like someone to be in charge who was so irrational and unpredictable. And yet, parents often behave in just as unpredictable and unjust kinds of ways.

I completely understand it, being a parent myself. Sometimes I am so physically tired that I don't feel like enforcing what I just told a child to do. I have learned, if I'm tired, I should make less commands at those moments. **Never command a child to do something that you're not prepared to go over and enforce what you just commanded.** Say things once, not three times and certainly not twenty times before you enforce the rule or the command. If you're not willing to follow through, don't even say it. Otherwise you're completely discrediting your word to your child and they will learn to ignore you. **Only say what you really mean, and if you say it, say it once. And once you've said it, follow through.** If you'll stick to these actions, as a parent, you will find life to be so much more pleasant for both you and your children because they'll soon learn that Mommy really means what she says, and "If Mama says it, I better do it." That might sound like a parent who is a dictator, but honestly, it's a life lesson your child needs to learn if they want to make it in a future job, or through a college class, or while driving a car, etc. **Following rules brings blessings and not following the rules brings consequences and learning this is vital to your child's long-term success and happiness. In the short term, it is a main key to peace and joy in the home.**

Not only that, but, think of the amount of time that you'd  save in your day if your kids did what you told them the first time you tell them. It's not really your child's fault that they don't obey. Brace yourselves for what I'm about to say because it's going to sting – it's generally the parent's fault when young children aren't in the habit of obeying. Be selective in what you ask them to do, but then follow through the first time with everything you say, and it won't take long to completely change the chaotic and tug-of-war atmosphere in your home. This can be one of the greatest gifts you can give your child and your entire family, not to mention everyone who comes in contact with your child in the future.)

Another reason that parents have a hard time providing necessary justice is because, well, we parents really do want to bring immediate joy to our children, so we don't like to give consequences. I get it! I want mine to be happy also. The problem is, if we are inconsistent in the boundaries -sometimes following through with consequences for crossing a boundary and the next time letting the same behavior go unpunished- this only brings confusion and breeds a wrong mentality in our children that if they "sneak around" or if they "beg enough" or "throw a big enough fit" Mom or Dad will eventually give in. When we do that, we are actually rewarding bad behavior. **If you reward it, they will repeat it.** Do you want them to be sneaky, manipulative, begging tantrum throwers? If you do want them to do those things, then go ahead and reward it by adjusting the standard in the moment and being inconsistent with justice. This will definitely produce more of those unpleasant (and unhealthy) behaviors. However, is this really what is BEST for your child?

Have you ever met an adult who didn't think the rules apply to them, or who is constantly trying to manipulate the system? How did that person get that way? Generally, it began when they were young, and no one took on the difficult but worthy task of putting a stop to that behavior and mentality in that child's life. I want blessing for my child's future, and I know that others will give them favor if they are being a blessing to those around them. On the other hand, if I reinforce in my child a selfish, "me first" mentality, I am setting them up for many unhappy days ahead. The best way is not usually the easy way, and this applies to providing justice for our child as well. I have met several people throughout my life who had some difficult self-centered years that resulted in many regrets and they often have attributed their selfish lifestyle to the fact that their parent "didn't care enough to give me consistent boundaries and consequences."

In fact, with my own adult children, I've had more than one of them come to me as a young adult and thank me for loving them enough to give them boundaries. **There is a sense of safety that a child receives from CONSISTENT, APPROPRIATE justice regarding their behavior. Be strong, Mama, in providing both LOVE and JUSTICE. It is worth it!**

That information was my not-so-short explanation of the first three rungs of the ladder climbing to God's Will for My Child's Life. (To read about the higher steps in the ladder, I write about that in some of my blog posts on raising older children).

Most mornings with my littles, when I would get up, it was these three ladder rungs that were on my mind. As I gave them a morning hug and got them breakfast I would think, "I need to give them a good start to their day of moving them up the ladder to God's will for their day." Routine doesn't have to be meaningless motions. You are raising God's artwork, helping them grow and bloom into the life that God has prepared for them.

As we help our children to develop a lifestyle of living out God's will for their lives, we want to especially fill their days with God Moments and God's Word (truth).

What do I mean by, "God Moments?" God Moments are the daily instances of seeing God at work in our lives and in the world around us, being tuned-in to "God with us." To achieve this lifestyle of seeing God and hearing from God in our kids' daily lives, we must intentionally train our children to see and hear God at work in throughout their day.

Examples of God-Moment-Living:

*Point out the <u>creativity of God</u> in our creation through our kids' five senses- seeing the beauty of a butterfly, the smell of a flower, the softness of the bunny's fur, or the sound of various birds singing.

*Identify the <u>goodness of God</u> as you experience something good in your day. James 1:17 says, "Every good and perfect gift is from above, coming down from the Father of the heavenly lights, who does not change like shifting shadows." Everything good that we receive is from God. As you develop the habit of reminding your children that throughout the day, when good things happen, you will be developing the habit in your children of recognizing God at work in their

lives. It is important for them to grasp this if they are to eventually reach the place of seeking God for daily decisions. Understanding that God is with us always, giving us good gifts and watching over us is a prerequisite for seeking Him for guidance in the direction of their lives as they get older. Habits today determines who we are tomorrow. **If we want them to rely on Him, we need to help them recognize Him.**

*When days are hard from big difficulties, let your children know that while your emotions are saying, "I'm scared" or "I'm disappointed" or "I'm broken-hearted" that those emotions are simply a physical response to situations, but that our heart truly knows that God is faithful, God is in control, God is good, and God is with us through the pain. I remember when we had moved to a new-to-us house, but our old house hadn't sold, and I was weary from financial concerns. Since I was crying almost daily for a few weeks, I knew that might potentially produce some feelings of insecurity in my kids to see their mama so worried (remember, rung #1, Safety Needs).

I also knew it was an opportunity for either building their relationship with and understanding of God OR it would diminish their trust in Him. They needed to know that I trusted God even when my emotions were showing otherwise. So, through my tears, I would say, "Kids, I know you see Mom crying and that probably makes you afraid. But there is nothing to fear as

God is with us and He is good. He will provide for all of our needs. Yes, my body is crying, but my soul is completely confident in our Heavenly Father, the Great Provider. It's fine to cry when you are sad or concerned but PRAY through the tears. Call out to God and thank Him for being with us."

Of course, God did eventually provide a buyer for our old house. I am confident that our kids learned, through

watching the process, that human emotions are part of life and that God, who is bigger than our emotions, God is worthy of our trust.

A word on entertainment for littles...

"Our children's minds are little sponges, soaking in and memorizing everything that is happening around them, so fill their time with meaningful wisdom and truth for life by being selective about the music, videos, conversations, and T.V. that is filling your home!

Right now, they are forming their understanding of how the world works - what attitudes are acceptable, what actions bring what results, the value of books, of laughter, of playing games.

These are the moments that matter. Don't squander them on empty, meaningless or even harmful "whatever's on right now" entertainment. There are so many great options for meaningful videos, music, and books available today.

Be intentional in your shaping of the moments lived by this precious little mind that you have been entrusted to develop. Don't settle for the empty, crude, "stinker-attitude" shows and books that has saturated our society. **Shape their minds and attitudes by being selective with their entertainment.**

CHAPTER 3: SCHEDULING YOUR LITTLE'S DAY

For being the tiniest bodies in the house, it's rather ironic that they can be so LOUD. How are we to get anything done with the other kids when the littlest of the bunch seems to demand our constant attention?! What is important when raising toddlers and preschoolers, helping them thrive, and keeping the chaos to a minimum? (*After all, no family can keep chaos away all the time but there are definitely things we can do to establish relative peace, help the whole family to be a blessing to others, and our home to be a joyful place to live.*) Let's take a look at the benefits of having a routine for our littles that brings a sense of peace and safety to their lives.

Children of all ages tend to be happier, better behaved, and quicker to learn from their environment when their day has a predictable schedule. If you want your child to thrive, give them the mental and emotional safety of a regular routine. In this section we will be

When Littles are Loud

looking at HOW TO SCHEDULE YOUR TODDLER/PRESCHOOLER'S DAY to help them flourish with a sense of peace and confidence!

GETTING A PLAN OF ACTION:

The schedule with my little tikes included a set time for the following activities in just 5 to 30-minute amounts. It may look like a lot of categories to do each day and you may be afraid that it will take up too much of your time as MOM, but I assure you, if you stick with it, after a little while, it will FREE YOU UP by greatly reducing the whining little person, tugging at your leg for love and attention because your toddler will learn to be busy with many of these activities on his own and you'll be free to focus on your older students' schoolwork or any of the other many obligations and, who knows you may even get to use the bathroom in peace once in a while! Or even, ...wait for it..., paint your nails, or something pampering like that!

Hey, a girl can dream, can't she?!

Once breakfast is finished each morning, just set a timer for the beginning of each hour to do one of these activities below. I kept the activities in the same order each day in an effort to build routine, and routine brings with it some peace and contentment that is hard to find otherwise.

At first, start with a small increment of time, such as 5 minutes per activity. If you keep it short, it keeps them "wanting more," which is a great way to help them look forward to it the

next day. This means the rest of each hour is available for their free play, which is also an important developmental need. Gradually your child will get used to the standard of behavior and the routine of the schedule. **That's when you'll see a happier, more content, self-entertaining child emerge where the demanding, cranky one once lived.**

HERE'S THE LIST OF ACTIVITIES I USED IN OUR LITTLES' DAILY ROUTINE. I'VE PUT AN * BESIDE EACH ACTIVITY THAT THE CHILD CAN EVENTUALLY DO ALONE.

Notice that I've alternated an "alone play" with a "non-alone play" time activity.

Keep all the items that are used in these activities reserved only for it's one special time each day. This is KEY to getting this plan to work effectively!!

Activities to Schedule

Bible Together Time
*Bible Alone Time
Bible Memory Verse Time
*Fine Motor Skills Time
Manners Time
*Activity Box Time
Chore Time
*Exercise Time
Math Basket Time
*Book Basket Time
Letters Basket Time
*Music Time
*Nature Time
*Nap Time

Bible Together Time

This is a very interactive time each day. Your toddler can sit on your lap (if you only have

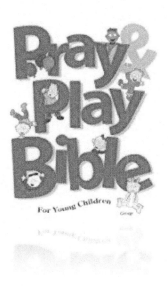

one or two) and you can snuggle while you read the Bible story, followed by a little prayer. Then you can sit on the floor together to sing a song or two or stand to do motions with your songs. Finally, you can move to the table to do a little craft, if you choose to do one. My favorite toddler Bible of all times is The Pray and Play Bible because it has big pictures to go with the story, finger play songs, little prayers, action songs, and even crafts that all go along with the story. During or after breakfast each weekday we'd begin our routine with BIBLE TOGETHER TIME - to set a priority in our lives that our time with God comes first.) It also gave me peace to know that even if the day may fall apart, at least we got our top priority done first thing in the morning. Remember to smile and laugh a lot with this activity – make it your child's favorite activity of the day!

Bible Alone Time

This was the second activity of our day and was completely different from Bible Together Time. A Bible story on a CD to listen to while they look at a kid's picture Bible or while they color Bible stories or play with Bible figures such as a Noah's Ark set. Fill their hearts with the Word of God while they are young and soaking in everything around them.

With Bible Alone Time you're helping your child develop the habit of daily spending time in the word of God with Jesus. They won't understand at first but as you continue this daily they, little by little, you will be instilling in your child the worldview that our great God loves us individually, personally, and wants to spend time with us each day. I don't know when it happens, but somewhere along the way, as the days go by, your little starts to comprehend our invisible God and develops a relationship with Him. Do you want God to be a marginal part of your child's life, or a constant anchor in their daily lives? How will you help to create that for them? Bible Alone Time was part of my strategy for doing this with my children.

Bible Memory Time

Spend a few minutes each day with your children memorizing scripture, and if they're little, use motions. My preference is to utilize a ABC scripture book to help with this (there are many on the market). We would memorize a verse for every letter of the alphabet, use sign language for the beginning letter and other motions on the key words to keep it fun and memorable. Young kids memorize things so much more easily than the rest of us. In fact, they are memorizing much of what they hear throughout the day, so DO pay attention to what radio station you listen to and what TV you are watching.

You would be surprised how young a child can be when they're ready to memorize scripture. If they're talking, they're ready! I began Bible Memory Time when my oldest two were 18 months and almost three. Within four months they BOTH had memorized a Bible verse for every letter of the alphabet. We would do motions to go along with the verses and they enjoyed it so much that they would ask to do it each day if I didn't lead it.

Be INTENTIONAL with this precious little heart and mind that you've been entrusted to raise!

Fine Motor Skills Time

Giving your toddler a set time to focus on small details such as how things fit together is great for mental development and can help with lengthening their attention span. (One of the worst things for limiting their development in this area is "screen time" - avoid it at all cost!! Okay, I might be a bit overly passionate about that, but there are many studies that show the harmful effects of too much screen time for all ages, but especially young children - from attention problems to sight development. It's long term harm for short term babysitting, and that's simply not worth it.)

Manners Time

This can start at a very early age (around nine months) by teaching them some infant sign language to express "eat, please" or "drink, please." (Their motor skills typically develop earlier than speech skills. If you don't teach them motions to express themselves, they will use screaming, tantrums, and whining to give

When Littles are Loud

you these messages. If you reward those behaviors, you are setting up a very unpleasant life for them and the whole family!) Manners, or "social skills" Time is so very valuable and the skills you teach them during this time each day can progress as they are developmentally able. Teach them to be gentle with the puppy or to not touch the doorknob or to ask before touching something that isn't theirs or to give a cheerful response. Manners Time is a great activity to continue for many years as your child's social comprehension increases. Teach them how to answer a phone, introduce two people, give a meaningful compliment, and so much more. One of the biggest determining factors in your child's social development, quality of relationships, and even job success hinges on how effective people skills your child develops over the years.

My favorite way for having Manners Time was usually to read a page from a book about a particular manner and then do some role-playing with that manner. Such as, "Okay,

Tori, you go up to the top of the stairs and I'm going to be downstairs in the kitchen. Listen for my voice, I'm going to call you. When you hear me call your name, you say, 'Coming

My grandson Jamey *roleplaying* some meal manners with stuffed animals.

Mom.' Say it cheerfully and loud enough for me to hear you. After you say that, you come

right downstairs quickly. Okay, let's give it a try." I'd make a game of this. Maybe give a high five when she got there or give her a sticker for doing it great. Then I'd say, "Okay, now you go out to the trampoline and listen for my voice..."We'd play the little game again from the trampoline. I was teaching her the appropriate way to respond. Just a few minutes of practice on this each day, along with some positive reinforcement, results in behavior that brings peace and contentment to a home.

Many years ago, I got lots of good ideas about manners from www.growingfamiliesusa.org. They have a small online bookstore of parenting books that I am thankful to have found all those years ago. Of course, there are no parenting books that we will ever agree with entirely, and these are no different, but my children's lives were enhanced, and our family had much more peace because of many of the ideas I got from those books.

There are lots of great Manners books, games, flashcards, stories... so many great tools available for developing content and pleasant little people.

Activity Box Time

Do you ever feel like you're going crazy from all the little pieces of toy collections that need to stay together but they are strung out all over the house? Hello, Activity Box salvation!

Look at your kid's toys that are little collections that would fit into a shoe box and would be a fun activity for your child. Contain each set and put them in a rotation for ACTIVITY BOX TIME.

When your child is very young, an ACTIVITY BOX contents could be something like Little People toys or colored stacking cups. When he's a bit older, such as a preschooler, this is a great time for smaller discovery items like **large** magnets (depending on age, **be safe of course**), sand with little soldiers or dinosaurs, crafts, matchbox cars, or Polly Pockets. I gave my toddlers a different activity box each day during ACTIVITY BOX TIME, with about 10-14 boxes in the rotation and reserving these boxes ONLY for ACTIVITY BOX TIME.

When Littles are Loud

Toddlers do ACTIVITY BOX Time in their high chair while pre-schoolers can be given a different specific location such as the kitchen table for this time slot. You don't want to give them freedom to run all over the house with these toys.

Activity Box Time is another opportunity in their day to teach them to focus and grow their attention span. This isn't a physically active play time, but a mentally active play time.

Chore Time

Emma is excited to learn how to clean the windows. She got plenty of paper towels! Looks like I need to teach her some portion control and enviromental caring.

(We now use hydrogen peroxide - safe for the kids and works so much better than expensive glass cleaner!)

"Seriously, you expect a toddler to have chores?" Well, yes, I do. Not because we parents will benefit from whatever chore we teach them at this age, but because your child needs:

1. A sense of accomplishment
2. To develop the habit of quality standards and work ethic

3. To have a mindset of a "Family is a Team and we all want to contribute to the team"

Chores at this age should be fun, but don't be afraid to teach them to do a chore to an appropriate degree of quality. For example, if his chore is to pick up the toys, give him the standard of "books go in this bin" and "toys go in this bin." Then YOU as parent need to stick to that standard. They will learn very early on if Mom means what she says or if she doesn't. **Be RELIABLE with your WORDS from** the very beginning of your relationship with them, if you want them to trust you.

Do you remember having a teacher growing up who would have strict standards one day and the next day she'd let you get away with things, then the next day she'd get upset with you for doing what she allowed the day before? You could never predict how you were supposed to behave or what she really meant. Did that feel like an environment where you could thrive? How about a teacher who was **strict but fair and loving**? Didn't that teacher inspire great things in you? Be

Reliable with Your Words and Be Dependable with Your Standards.

One of my favorite toddler chores to assign, is to give a baby wipe or wash cloth to the toddler and have him or her wash something - some of his toys or her play table, etc. A way to teach them quality with this might be to say, "Now don't miss any spots. Make ALL of it shine!" Start the habit of quality work while they are young and let them know they're an important part of the family team! Yay!!

I usually had EXERCISE Time twice a day for preschoolers. Of course, littles play actively all day long, but only two times a day was it this specific, structured EXERCISE TIME.

Here's what you do:

Get some Popsicle Sticks or any little item that you can write on. Write a different activity on each stick such as "Trampoline," Trike," "Sidewalk Chalk," "Swing set," "Balls," etc.

Have your child draw out one stick. That's the

exercise they'll do today for this time-slot. I didn't give them a choice during this time because it's good for them to have some times every day where they don't get to make their own choice. It's great to give them freedom to choose plenty of things, but **it is also a necessary character quality for your child to grow up knowing that "we can be happy even when the choice isn't ours to make."** If you think about well-adjusted, successful adults, they have to do things all the time that they wouldn't CHOOSE to do, but still NEED to do. It's great to create scenarios to develop this necessary character quality in your child.

Math Basket Time

Get a crate and start collecting different number/math manipulatives and math games at garage sales or from Pinterest, for example. Once a day, at "MATH BASKET TIME", have your child pick something from the crate to "play numbers." In the early days the crate will have number blocks, number puzzles, counting monkeys, number picture books, an abacus, etc.

 As your child gets older and their skills progress, the items in the math crate will change with the child, continuing all the way through multiplication, division, and fractions, as there are great math manipulatives for all these concepts.

My eight-year-old still has a "Math Basket Time" each day in addition to her math schoolwork. The items in the basket have changed over the years, but the timeslot still exists in her life. For example, my eight-year-old's "Math Basket" now includes multiplication wrap-ups, a little math electronics game, a couple different math games, fraction overlays, etc.

Book Basket Time

This is a great planned activity for all those library books that you bring home each week. The first part of BOOK TIME is with

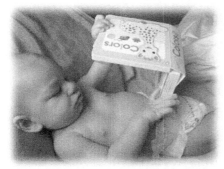

mommy, then the second half of this activity is ALONE BOOK TIME.

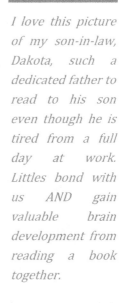

I love this picture of my son-in-law, Dakota, such a dedicated father to read to his son even though he is tired from a full day at work. Littles bond with us AND gain valuable brain development from reading a book together.

Sit and read one or two books with him. Then give him 2-3 books from the basket for his alone book time. Set a timer for 5-30 minutes (depending on your child's age and ability -start with a small

amount of time). Get him a cozy place to read, such as on a bean bag or a blanket spread on the floor - a special place for his daily reading time. He should stay in that spot until the timer dings (start out with a very short number of minutes). Then teach him to put the picture books back in the basket.

Teach your child to take good care of the books, not to tear, throw, or step on them. Having this type of focused play followed by cleanup of that play, will teach him great habits for future academics and orderliness... Ahhh, breathe a sigh of relief that you are teaching your child to not be scattered and chaotic.

Little brother, Asher, having Blanket Time while his big brother is having Book Basket Time.

Letters Basket Time

Get a crate or box or basket and start collecting different phonics manipulatives (ABC blocks or letter magnets to play with on the fridge, for example) and phonics games. There's so many you can find at garage sales, used bookstores, or homeschool curriculum fairs. Each day at this time, spend a few minutes teaching them about letters and sounds then set the timer for their alone play

When Littles are Loud

with one of the letters toy sets. My very favorite phonics tool that was the first step in teaching my kids to read, was a very simple CD and paper from Discovery Toys called "Sounds Like Learning."

We'd sit on a special spot on the floor each day for this. The CD would play, I'd hold the little paper that goes with the CD containing the letters and pictures of what is being sung, and I'd hold my child's finger and teach him or her to point to each sound as we'd sing the song together. Then, after weeks of us doing this, he would be pointing by himself, as he followed along with the song, singing it. Eventually, he would be able to sit there by himself singing the song, pointing to the letters and pictures. So, that became something he did by himself and I would teach him the next step in reading, using Abeka's My Blend and Word Book (www.abeka.com).

I would spend just a few minutes teaching reading skills, then set the timer for his alone play with the Letters Basket in our special spot for LETTER BASKET Time. (I would pick out one or two items from the Letters Basket for him to have while the timer was going. I didn't give him free reign over the entire basket of items or it wouldn't stay exciting and special each day. Rotating the manipulatives is key to all of these special activities, to hold their attention.)

This cd is from CedarmontKids.com, which has lots of great audio options. I also really like The Donut Man and Seeds Family Worship

Music Time

My kids always loved this time the most of all -Educational songs, Bible Songs, Praise Songs... that a child listens to while playing with building blocks or dolls, etc. If they were not old enough to play unsupervised in their room, I would have them spend MUSIC TIME in their playpen with 3-4 toys that would switch each day but if they were safe in their room alone, this was their bedroom alone play time. Alone play is an important part of their development as it teaches them that their contentment is not dependent on any other person. If you have a child you is very clingy,

never letting you out of their sight, you will find this alone play time very beneficial to helping them overcome that need for your presence to be the source of their contentment. (For older pre-schoolers or elementary age children, I personally like the learning songs by Claritas Publishing, found at https://crossseven.org?ap_id=pracitcallyspe akingmom.com (This is an affiliate link.)

This website, www.crossseven.org, is something my family has used for the last five years. Daily, my elementary children (my youngest is in fourth grade, so only one elementary child now), watch these short memory song videos that introduce a new memory song each week for the following categories: Bible, Geography, Latin, Math, Language, Science, History, and Hymns. By the end of a school year they have learned a huge amount just from their musical memory time.

In the toddler years, I loved to have them listen to songs that teach manners, safety, and Bible stories. Sometimes I made my own recordings to tell them things I wanted them to know, such as, "Tori, Mom and Dad love you so much. We're very proud of you for how you share with others, and smile when someone says, 'hello' to you. Let's sing Mommy's favorite hymn, 'What a Friend We Have in Jesus...' There are lots and lots of great educational and Bible songs CDs these days. Don't waste this precious season of their lives just listening to Disney songs, etc. Sure, those are fine, but our children's minds are little sponges, soaking in and memorizing everything right now, so fill their time with meaningful wisdom and truth for life!

This is a picture of our daughter, Becca, the mother of the boys in many of the pictures in this book. She actually implements this type of schedule with her boys as well. When I was recently there for a visit she told Jamey, 15 months, that it was time for music time. He fussed for a few seconds because he

was having fun with his relatives, but she was really wanting him to learn this routine, so she stuck with the daily schedule. He fussed at first that he had to stop playing with his aunt (our youngest daughters Emma and Abby), but within a minute, he was happily playing in his playpen while listening to learning songs. It was a precious picture of the contentment and peace that can come to a home that has learned to schedule their day. A little key to making this work well is to put the playpen in a separate room from where you are. Becca put the playpen in a room where no one was so he could have his music time alone – because this time slot is equally teaching alone play as well as the educational concepts in the songs.

Nature Time

Sunshine, fresh air, the sound of birds, dirt to dig in, bugs to find... these are so important for our child's development. If the weather permits, make sure they get daily outside play time. This is a good time for you to refresh as well - work in your flower bed while they play in the dirt or soak your feet in the kiddie pool your kiddie is playing in. I have this activity marked as an "alone play" activity because they do not need entertaining when they play outside. Of course, all of these activities still require safety supervision for little people.

If the weather doesn't allow outside play, you'll have to be a little creative to bring some nature inside.

Nap Time

I'm sure I didn't need to mention this timeslot, as every mama knows that her little needs at least one nap time per day. I would encourage you to REST WHEN YOUR LITTLE  RESTS. Don't feel guilty about taking a nap or at least kicking back in the recliner and listen to a meaningful podcast or some calm music. Moms of littles really need breaks just as much as our littles do! When my littles would nap, I'd have the olders spend quiet time in their rooms as well. They could read or work on homework or journal, but they were to stay quiet because **Little and Her Mama need rest**!

When the timer goes off each hour, do that hour's activity with your toddler or preschooler. The first few days it may be a bit of a wrestling match to get your little person used to staying put until the timer goes off but do keep trying. In a few days you will begin to experience more smiles and less fussiness. Kids really do flourish and thrive with a predictable routine that encourages development of body and mind and character.

Tips for Implementing Your New Toddler Schedule:

*Keep each of the special activity items reserved to be used **ONLY during that activitiy** and, with most of the activities, **ROTATE the items** used to keep the activities exciting and something for your little tike to look forward to each day. Variety is the spice of life, even for littles!

*I would NOT attempt to implement all these activities at once. Pick the one you feel would be most beneficial for your family, your child, and for you right now. Then start with that one activity. Add in another one in a few days, and so on.

*As much as possible, keep the activities in the same order each day. **Routine** brings a sense of safety to children.

*Be prepared for a STRUGGLE as you implement each new activitiy. New habits are difficult to develop for every age person, including littles. You've got to be stronger in this battle than your little! It is for her sake but she is too young to comprehend the benefits of routine, of learning these different mental improvements, and the character development that comes with these activities. **It is worth the effort, Mama.** For many years ahead there will be different difficult obstacles and power struggles that you'll encounter with your child. **God gave that child YOU because your child needs someone who does what is BEST for him or her, not what is easy or what gives immediate pleasure.** Your job is to be aware of the big picture, your child's future, and then insist on what is best for her. If children were capable of deciding what was best for themselves,

God would've made a different life system in which children raise themselves without parents. That's not the system He made because it is not what's best for our kids. Be an example to them of doing what is BEST instead of doing what is EASY. As each of my children has entered the high school years, my husband has had a theme for those four years – "Lead your heart, don't follow your heart." This concept is the opposite of what society tells us. **All around us we hear the message to "let your heart be your guide" but the truth is that our hearts are easily swayed, emotionally charged, and irrational. We need to lead our hearts.** God tells us in Proverbs 22:15 that "Folly is bound up in the heart of a child..." and in Jeremiah 17:9, "the heart is deceitful above all things..." (NKJV). **Teach your children to lead their hearts with truth, not be swayed this way and that way based on the irrational whims and emotional pulls of the heart. Teaching them this begins at a very young age. Even as crawlers and toddlers and preschoolers, they can learn that if what we want isn't what's best for us, then we should still do what is best, not what is easy or comfortable.**

Chapter 4: The Little Imitator Lives Here

Life with Littles can be exhilarating and exhausting! Parents need a plan for living successfully with these tiny humans! Our plan has three parts:

First things first – focusing on LOVE, JUSTICE, SAFETY, and PHYSICAL NEEDS

1. Developing a ROUTINE for increasing peace and priorities.
2. Recognizing that, since the little imitator lives here, we must lead in allowing God to lead us. Our children are our great opportunity, given by God, to motivate us to change for the better. Let's look now at this third part of the plan.

In this final section of <u>When Littles Are Loud</u> we will face the reality that these small humans are IMITATING US. Yikes! Quick warning, here: It might get just a little uncomfortable as we examine....hmm how shall I say this.... your HEART. In fact, I'm going to tell you that IF you're a big mess on the inside (which most of us are), there's very slim possibility that you can hide that fact from your little person for much longer. That toddling little tike is going to turn into a talking two-year-old and, in a blink, your offspring will have become a little kid. There's something you should know about kids - they can see the real you. Their little eyes peer right through your mask and see your heart.

Our middle three children are all boys. Each of them spent some amount of energy and focus in their younger years trying to imitate their dad. It was so cute - the ways they'd try to do what their dad was doing. Our son Nathan had a toy saxophone and he would play it – bending forward then bending back, just like his daddy would do when playing the saxophone every Sunday at church.

Our youngest son, Andrew, as a little guy, would come to me every Saturday evening and whisper to me, "What's Daddy wearing to church tomorrow?" I would show him something  *Our son Andrew* from my husband's closet and Andrew would scurry off, disappearing for a while. He would re-emerge a little bit later carrying some clothes. "Mom, will these match Daddy?" Or he would sometimes ask me, "Mom, can you buy me a tie like Daddy's tie?" On Sunday mornings you'd see him come out with a big beaming grin on his face, as he had set a goal and achieved it – dressing for church, just like Daddy. You see that grin in the picture? That was our little Andrew at the age I've described to you.

You know, those little guys don't stay little very long, but the values and worldview that they develop at that young age stays with them. Andrew actually still loves to dress up in a suit. He's a junior in high school and this year he spent a week at our state capitol as part of an organization called TeenPact (an organization for Christian youth to develop citizen leadership). He spent four days in a suit and tie interacting with legislators and their constituents, discussing the needs of the people. He also has spent time in a speech and debate organization that requires a suit and tie for competitions. Believe it or not, even as a young man, he enjoys how he feels when he looks professional. When your little ones are imitating you, are they developing habits that are going to help or hinder their future?

No matter how many littles live at your house, each bundle of joy comes with lots of entertaining moments, tiring moments, proud moments, and totally INSANE moments too.

When Littles are Loud

One thing is for sure: each
child changes
everything forever!

**Here is the story of your
little imitator...**

Not that long ago you were anticipating the arrival of that precious little one. You knew he would come with a fair share of difficulties, but you also knew that becoming a parent was going to be the most awesome experience of your life!

After all, you could already feel your heart expanding, making room for this new, mysterious, miraculous creation!

He arrives, and your heart feels like it could burst with love for this precious, helpless human.

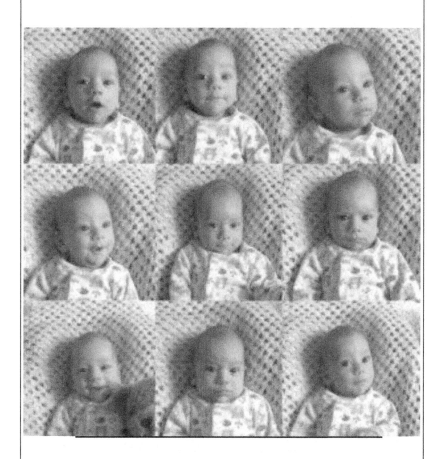

Oh, the many faces of the moments that follow as you get to know this little guy. Sweet bliss!

_____

_____

Reality check!! - He's adorable but YOU are EXHAUSTED.

Now, the lovely wedding day is a faint memory

Our daughter, Becca, and her husband, Dakota.

and it has given way to....uhh...

...the crazed fear and dismay of parenting a two-year-old!

He makes big messes

And if you've got multiple little people, even grocery shopping is complicated.

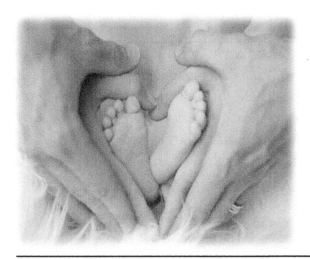

Have you ever wondered why God designed these little ones to grow up under a parent's care? I mean, they could have been born full-grown and independent. Or they could've hatched from an egg and never met their mom. But that's not how God designed this mini-human to grow. No, quite the opposite.

He made this precious bundle totally dependent on US, the parents. Seriously? I mean, we adults are all kind of a mess in the selfishness department! Why would God do this?!

I don't know about you, but I have yet to meet someone who is really prepared for parenthood. You know why that is?

We aren't ready for parenthood because we can't even begin to comprehend the concept of loving that deeply, that selflessly, that sacrificially until we hold that priceless treasure in our arms.

We stare at that little face, experience those tiny little fingers wrapped around our finger and we

know, this is it. This is no dress rehearsal; it's the real deal. This little one will be shaped by who I choose to be right no. And this little one deserves so much more than what I am capable of being on my own.

For a while we're so distracted by all the newness and responsibilities (and exhaustion) and joy of parenting that we are able to tuck away that nagging reality that we alone are not enough for

this little one. But pretty soon as the newness wears away and as the complications of life come stronger, we are faced with a choice.

Who am I going to be?

God's been wanting us to ask this question for a long time, but we weren't ready to listen. Up until now we had managed to push Him away. It's actually not that pretty of a picture at that moment because we feel like throwing our hands up and saying, *"Wow, not only do I stink at parenting, in fact, I kind of just stink at life!"*

But our love for this tiny-yet-giant responsibility holds every ounce of our heart and we seek to be better for our child's sake and we step towards our Heavenly Father and ask Him to lead us.

<u>And there it is!</u> Now we arrive at the exact pivotal moment that matters most! Our wildly intentional Creator wanted us to realize our need for HIM and His desire for us to be in a deep, meaningful relationship with Him. *Do you think, when your child is older, if she keeps her distance from you emotionally and your relationship becomes just surface, wouldn't that break your heart? It breaks our Heavenly Father's heart when we keep our distance from Him.* There's so much guidance and peace and future with Him that He longs to bring to our life, if we will let Him.

For some of us extra-stubborn adults (such as myself), **those adorable little handfuls are the only force in creation strong enough to motivate us to transform from a "selfish human" into an "I-love-this-little-guy-more-than-I-love-my-(habits, hangups, reoccurring selfish choices)-human."**

You see, we're all pretty messed up. But God

is a gentleman; He's not going to force us to change if we don't want to. IF we are willing, He will help us change. **And it is this little treasure that we have been entrusted with that is the motivation we needed to turn to our Heavenly Father to bring us the abundant life we had been missing.**

So, he sends these little adorable people to reveal ourselves to us. And then He does the UNTHINKABLE!! - **He designs them to IMITATE our every word and action.**

Do you realize you're being watched?

The reality is, that no matter which choice you make at that critical moment in your parenting journey (or, now for me, grandparenting journey), whether you decide to turn to God for His strength and wisdom, and finally realize that His ways are better than your ways, or whether you keep right on pushing Him away, either way your little one is YOUR great IMITATOR.

She adores you!
She wants to be just like you!
And she studies your actions
and reads your heart
and does likewise.

Your attitudes...
your habits...
your passions...
even your choices...

he is imitating you.

What you do, he wants to do.
What you value, he values.
Who you disrespect, he disrespects.
And what you ignore, most likely, so will he.

So, parent (or grandparent)...
what do you value?
what are you choosing?

Your little doesn't need a perfect parent (those don't exist), but what he or she needs is three main ingredients to flourish and thrive under your care:

1. Littles need lots of love-tank filling daily with an equal measure of consistent justice.
2. They need a sense of safety that consistency provides -providing for their physical and emotional needs.
3. Littles need parents who recognize their need for their Heavenly Father, who let Him into their heart in a big, all out "transform-me-completely-God" kind of way. They need you to lead in choosing to let Him lead in all things.

Our children are our great opportunity to turn over the running of our life to our Heavenly Father, for their sake and ours. And, in so doing, we become the person

that God wanted us to be all along, so that they have a better opportunity to choose well also.

Don't waste
this great moment,
for a little one
is depending on you
to choose well.

Our daughter Abby

Ephesians 5:1
"Therefore be imitators of God, as beloved children. And walk in love, as Christ loved us and gave himself up for us, a fragrant offering and sacrifice to God"(NIV)

MEET THE PRACTICALLY SPEAKING MOM

Val is blessed to be wife of Rich for 26 years, mom to seven children (including two married daughters and their husbands), homeschool mom for 20 years, Grandma to two perfect grandsons, speaker, and a speech teacher for homeschool co-

ops.

"While my greatest desire is to serve my Lord Jesus, one of my greatest passions is encouraging parents to build strong families and to seek a life of excellence! I enjoy speaking at women's groups, parenting conferences, and home school conventions where I seek to share

practical advice through a "tell it like it is" style with a little humor and wisdom –wisdom that I've only gained through all the many mom-fails and follies. Thankfully God's grace fills in the gaps where our abilities fall short!

With a degree in Speech Communications, I have enjoyed teaching Speech classes for the past 18 years to help students develop their speaking skills for both public and interpersonal settings (such as interview prep and conflict resolution) through fun and practical interactive exercises. From manners to drama games to conflict resolution strategies, mock job interviews, and college speech prep, I thrive on motivating students to communicate effectively, sincerely and for God's glory! If you'd like to get to know me better or see more of my student curriculum, visit my website, www.PracticallySpeakingMOM.com and follow me on Facebook, "Val Harrison, The Practically Speaking MOM."

My prayer is that the words of my mouth and the thoughts of my heart would be pleasing in His sight for He is my Rock and my Redeemer! (Psalm 19:14)

PracticallySpeakingMOM.com

Practically **Speaking**

...words of my mouth and meditation of my heart...

From the Series "Our Family God's Masterpiece"

Wearing All Your Hats without Wearing Out

From Chores to Character Issues to Chaos Control

Finding Your Focus for Your Family to be the Masterpiece God Intended It to Be

Gaining
Momentum

Preparing Your Student for the Pursuit of a
Career with or without College

Val Harrison

Follow Val on Facebook: Val Harrison, The Practically
Speaking MOM and on Instagram PracticallySpeakingMOM